Wilhelm Haller

The People of God and the Politics of Jesus in Society and Economy

Essays by Wilhelm Haller

The People of God and the Politics of Jesus in
Society and Economy
© 1974-2014 Wilhelm Haller

Texianer Verlag
for the Hugh & Helene Schonfield World
Service Trust
Johannesstrasse 12, D-78609 Tuningen,
Deutschland
www.texianer.com

ISBN: 978-3-949197-93-2

Translated from the German by
© 2022 Stephen A. Engelking

About the Author

Wilhelm (Willi) Haller (*25. Juli 1935; † 2. August 2004) was not a theologian but an industrialist. Within the framework of his commitment to the Fellowship of Reconciliation, he also lectured on theological topics. He is mainly known for his contribution to the humanization of work but he was much concerned with philosophical and religious issues. He was very much influenced by the teachings of the bible scholar and Messianist Hugh J. Schonfield and convinced that a Servant Nation was the only way to solve the fundamental problems of mankind. He not only founded the leading flexible working hours and security equipment company, *Interflex*, but also was instrumental in innovative social projects. An unbelievable entrepreneur (most of his initiatives are still operating today), he was a gentle approachable person and father of four children.

Apart from authoring a number of books, he was a contributor to many magazines and periodicals. Some of these writings have been preserved and are presented here as a collection for the reader who is prepared to challenge his own ideas.

From Wikipedia.org:

"His ideas and concepts caused him to be known as the "father of Flexitime" and led to the discussion on making working hours flexible be discussed across the then West Germany, and with time to find more and more implementation. Haller advocated "three for two" job sharing to combat unemployment in the late 1970s. His advice was in demand as a Flexitime expert, not only in Germany but also worldwide.

In the course of this development, Haller started to design the first computer system worldwide from which a little later the first PC-based time recording equipment for SME's (small to medium-sized businesses) were developed. In their basic mode of operation, these systems met the standards of all time recording systems today. Many other products and patents can be attributed to Haller's inventions.

In order to achieve his goals faster and better and to give the employees a share in the success, Haller founded the company *Interflex Datensysteme* with three others of like mind which continually developed to become European market leader (it was later taken over by Ingersoll Rand). Haller built his organization on the basis of progressive management concepts. Employee motivation played a central role in this. The idea was that one third of profits should be shared each by investors, employees and charitable projects. A novelty for that time was the active involvement of employees in decision making processes.

Haller never saw himself as the boss but rather as part of a team, yet he was nevertheless a recognized and competent CEO. He was able to make his ideas understood and related them to others, inspiring and exciting his employees, winning them for a shared vision, and thus using their knowledge potential for the organization. It was extremely important for Haller for work to be fun.

Willi Haller left his company in the 1980s and worked as a consultant and coach in companies, trade unions, institutions and social organizations. He founded a number of social projects, including the "Lebens House" and the "Nudel House". He was guest speaker at universities and management seminars and appeared in television shows.

Although Haller was a radical thinker, he also had an influence on leading managers because he was not only charismatic but also pragmatic and logical in his argumentation. He is the author of a number of books and many articles about management, economy and theological themes. He saw himself as the student of the philosopher Martin Buber, whose influence is apparent in Haller's book The Dark Fire demonstrated in this extract:

> *...the process of transformation of the seed into fruit – to use an image of Jesus – the darkness of the earth and its apparent annihilation are decisive. Obviously, salvation grows above all out of sorrowful experience with oneself and with the environment.*

Haller's ideas continue to be a source of influence even after his death, including in the work of the International Leadership and Business Society, which has set as its aim the humanizing of work."

Contents

About the Author..3

The "People of God" Concept......................9

The Politics of Jesus..33

Dualism and polarity..49

Might and Power...53

Money, Community and Property.................59

Unemployment..67

Flexible Working Hours....................................71

The Human Job..75

Solidarity—the Price of Future Employment......83

The *Lebenshaus* in Trossingen.........................93

The Pioneer Society..103

A Last Thought..107

More Books in English by Wilhelm Haller........109

The "People of God" Concept

Those who are familiar with the series *Texts for Reflection* from the Herder Library will learn that "in the deeper layers of the soul, all people are related to each other", as it states in the preface.

We recognize more and more that God has revealed and is revealing himself at all times and in all cultures. Obviously, throughout the traditions of all religions, the gift of knowing and experiencing God is to be found, even if it is mingled everywhere with the sands of meager humanity, as shaped by the spirit of each age and culture. And yet, for most of us, our ancestral religion rightly remains the house in which we feel at home, even if we must painfully recognize "that every religion is an exile, but an exile into which God has sent us", as Martin Buber puts it.

Does the Judeo-Christian tradition, the

Christian religion, now have a special significance, taking this realization into account — without thereby elevating it above the other religions — focal points which, as essential elements, complement the contributions of the other religions to an overall picture valid for all humanity?

If this is so — and I am personally convinced of it — then it is the emphasis on liberation, on redemption, which characterizes the Judeo-Christian tradition, whereby this liberation is always to be experienced on an evolutionary path, the path of salvation history, of history shaped by God.

Thus, a political-spiritual body, namely the so-called people of God, is to be, as it were, the followers of the priestly King Jesus (insofar as he is recognized as the Christ, i.e. as the Messiah, the King anointed by God for this task). They should be the advance guard of all mankind and show the way and direction, so that "His kingdom shall come" and also become outwardly visible on this earth. The span of the Bible reaches from the Garden of Eden, the starting point of human development, to the heavenly-earthly Jerusalem — its goal.

The guiding theme of the Bible is the message of liberation. "I am your God who sets you free", as it says in Moses. Meaning: "I have brought you out of slavery, and I promise liberation from every form of internal and external enslavement, liberation from all bondage and that to everyone who turns to me".

Hence the merciless condemnation of every form of idolatry in the Old Testament, because idolatry always leads to enslavement. We often fail to understand how the ancient Israelites could pay homage to various idols. We fail to realize that we do the same. The idols today merely have different names, such as prosperity, progress, security, career, prestige, sex, alcohol, etc.

In the New Testament and in the Christianity of the centuries behind us, there is a shift in emphasis. Nevertheless, if we take a closer look and neglect certain aberrations, it becomes clear that the core message remains the same, even if new terms such as "the redemption from sins" etc. have come to the fore. As valid as ever: "I am your God who shall set you free".

For the ancient Israelites, however, this message of liberation was not only a message but a concrete historical experience: liberation from slavery in Egypt, renunciation of the secure flesh pots of the life of slavery, acceptance (even if grumbling) of the unsecured meager bread of freedom, decades of wanderings in the wilderness and finally the arrival in the promised land. This historical experience of ancient Israel should be symbolic of the path and history of man, for the individual, for the peoples and for all humanity.

The ancient Israelites recognized this and also saw in it an obligation to convey this message of liberation and freedom to the peoples of the world through the exemplary realization of this policy of God both on a small and a large scale, in domestic and foreign policy. The way to this goal should not be an end in itself but an example for the other peoples, so that they would be able to understand it.

In Isaiah this is clearly expressed:

To the tribes of the world I give you for a light, that my freedom may reach to the edge of the earth.

Consequently, it becomes clear that the realization of God's policy of freedom, peace and justice among the "world tribes", i.e. among the other peoples of this world, depends on its realization by the People of God being carried out in an exemplary and visible way. The redemption of the peoples of this world

The "People of God" Concept

and of the whole creation depends on the "revelation of the children of God" (Paul) and on the fact that the people of God become manifest, stand up, realize and carry out their task and thus become "a light to enlighten the Gentiles". Micah and Isaiah describe this goal in almost the same words in a magnificent vision:

> *And it shall come to pass in the last days,*
> *that the mountain of the Lord's house*
> *shall be established in the top of the*
> *mountains,*
> *and shall be exalted above the hills;*
> **and all nations shall flow unto it.**
> **And many people shall go**
> *and say, Come ye, and let us go up to the*
> *mountain of the Lord,*
> *to the house of the God of Jacob;*
> *and he will teach us of his ways,*
> *and we will walk in his paths:*
> **for out of Zion shall go forth the law,**
> **and the word of the Lord from**
> **Jerusalem.**
> *And he shall judge among the nations,*
> *and shall rebuke many people:*
> *and they shall beat their swords into*
> *plowshares,*
> *and their spears into pruninghooks:*
> *nation shall not lift up sword against nation,*

neither shall they learn war any more.

......

It is astonishing and surprising that we have so completely overlooked and continue to overlook the central importance of the example that God's people have to give to the other peoples of this world in order to redeem them from their hopeless entanglements in imperialism, the politics of force and violence. Otherwise, we would not be constantly laboriously endeavoring hopelessly, to get our respective nation-states—as Germans the Federal Republic or the GDR, as Americans the U.S., etc.—to implement a policy such as that advocated by Jesus, i.e. a policy of freedom, peace and justice. This effort is indeed courageous and admirable, but from a biblical point of view it is hopeless, because the "world tribes", i.e. our nation states, will only try to realize such a policy when God's people have concretely demonstrated to them the practical feasibility of such a policy. Thus, for us in the international peace movement, insofar as we align ourselves with the Judeo-Christian tradition, it cannot be primarily a matter of convincing our respective governments in Bonn, East Berlin, Washington, etc., of the practicability of Jesus' policy. Rather, our concern should

The "People of God" Concept 15

be to rally God's people and collectively set about fulfilling his task. This is what Jesus intended. For this reason, he also sent his disciples only to the Jews and expressly forbade them to get involved with non-Jews.

This did not happen because he wanted to deliver them mercilessly to eternal damnation. Rather, he knew that as the Messiah he could only bring salvation to the world through his followers, the people of God. The individual Messiah thus needed the discipleship of the collective Messiah. His compatriots did not understand him at that time, therefore only the way of the cross remained for him. Only very few of his Christian followers through the centuries have understood him. And so the Messiah Jesus of Nazareth, the priestly king of God's people, stands to this day without a following that would be willing to implement his policies without reservation. And the peoples of this world are still waiting in vain for the example that will inspire them to follow.

So the world today stands on the precipice of global catastrophe, not because there is a Reagan, a Kohl, a Strauss and an Andropov, but because we are exhausting ourselves in criticizing the policies of these people instead of constructively committing ourselves to the work of reconstruction, as had been demanded again and again by the prophets of old:

> *"Hearken unto me, my people; and give ear unto me, O my nation: for a law shall proceed from me, and I will make my judgment to rest for a light of the people. My righteousness is near; my salvation is gone forth, and mine arms shall judge the people; the isles shall wait upon me, and on mine arm shall they trust." (Jes. 51)*
>
> *Wake up, wake up,*
> *Clear a path!*
> *Take away what causes to stumble,*
> *from the way of my people! (Jes. 57)*
>
> *Arise,*
> *shine,*
> *for your light has come,*
> *HIS glory,*
> *has shone above you. (Jes. 60)*
>
> *Go through, go through the gates; prepare ye the way of the people; cast up, cast up the highway; gather out the stones; lift up a standard for the people.*
>
> *Behold, the Lord hath proclaimed unto the*

> *end of the world, Say ye to the daughter of Zion, Behold, thy salvation [freedom] cometh; behold, his reward is with him, and his work before him. (Jes. 62)*

However, not only is the great call found in Isaiah, but also promise and great consolation:

> *And it shall come to pass, that before they call, I will answer; and while they are yet speaking, I will hear.(Jes. 65)*

> *For thus saith the LORD, Behold, I will extend peace to her like a river... (Jes. 66)*

What does this development work consist of in concrete terms?

Martin Buber once put it this way:

> *No one can serve God perfectly except a people. For the service of God is called justice, and all the righteousness of individuals can only provide stones for building, but a people can build justice. This is what Isaiah means: Do not intertwine your lot with the unrighteousness of your neighbors, but build up justice with your own lives, and the love of the nations will fly to you, and you will be a blessing on earth.*

So we should not intertwine our lives with the injustice of the powerful, but in the spirit of Jesus' politics go the way of absolute powerlessness, even renouncing passive resistance. However, we should not condone grievances and injustices and not help to sweep them under the carpet, but rather, in the spirit of Gandhi, make conflicts and problems visible. In Jesus-style politics, however, non-cooperation would take the place of non-violent resistance (with Buber: *Do not intertwine your lot...*). This is the refusal of loyalty that the state demands of us, wherever the demanded loyalty is in contradiction with a reverence for life — put in general terms. This refusal of loyalty appears at first as a purely negative step. It would be, too, if it were not connected with the self-commitment to build justice with our own lives, individually and collectively. Collectively, so that the people can come into being, which, according to Buber, can build justice. And a people comes into being when more and more people join together to form a community, provide this community with the loyalty that they have withdrawn from their state, and in this way give this community autonomy.

The people of God should therefore be, expressed in a contemporary and non-religious way, a world-spanning, i.e. cross-border autonomous community of people who make it their task to put the politics of Jesus into practice, without presupposing membership of any religious community.

God's people do not need their own territory. Therein lies the error of the Jews when they established the nation-state of Israel. Just as the tribe of Levi as the priestly tribe of the people of Israel was not allowed to have a property, the people of God is not allowed to have a territory, because what the tribe of Levi was for Israel, the people of God is for the world (*You shall be to me a people, of priests* — with Moses). Speaking practically (God is a politician in real terms!), inconceivable that a people, which has to protect a territory, that is property and privileges, can put into practice the policy of Jesus. The realization of the politics of Jesus can be only be carried out by a people that has no territory to protect. Just as the prototype of a new machine is not placed in a customer's factory for testing, but is, as it were, tested under careful conditions in the laboratory, so the revolutionary new policy of Jesus must first be implemented in laboratory fashion, that is, by a people without territory and without riches. The hurdles for implementation must not be too high. Francis of Assisi had already recognized this when he refused to take possession. He said, *Then we would need weapons to defend them.* And in doing so, he would betray his Lord.

The people of God also do not need a uniform religion. So today it is less about a dogmatized and ritualized Christianity than about a practiced Christianity. Here the limits of the official churches are demonstrated, as the Abbot Joachim of Fiore already did almost a thousand years ago in his *Eternal Gospel* (quoted from Adolf Holl *Der letzte Christ*):

> *The mysteries of the biblical scriptures point us to three states.*
> *To the first, we were under the law.*
> *To the second, where we stand in grace.*
> *To the third, so close already, where love will reign, once and for all.*
> ……
>
> *The first state is called the Old Testament, where we were servants. The second state is called the New Testament, where we were like dependent sons. In the third state, we will be free.*
> *The first state was under the Father's regime. The second state was under the sign of the Son. In the third state, the Holy Spirit will blow wherever He wants.*

> ....
> *The first state corresponds to the simplicity of children, the second to the knowledge of man, the third to the wisdom of age.*
> ....
> *Now the Holy Church, like the woman in the Apocalypse, lies crying in her travail. What is to come out of her will be called the spiritual people. When the time comes for the kingdom of love to be established, the riddles and signs that have been spoken to us so far will turn into the full understanding of things. Baptism and the Lord's Supper will then be superfluous, and also the administrators of the sacraments, the priesthood in its well-ordered hierarchy, will be relieved of their obligations, because then the spirit will speak to the hearts of the people without the intervention of authorities, inspiring them to live in harmony. Will the sanctified order of priests be grieved that it must cease when the spirit church dawns? No, never, never shall Peter's successors turn green with envy that they have to give way to the new order of the spirit.*

It seems to me that the time is ripe for the fulfillment of Joachim's vision. The danger of global destruction through human hubris is only too real. But we also know from Goethe *Where danger grows, so does that which can save.*

Oddly enough, a game with the numbers of the years also seems to signal a time of change:

According to a calculation made by the Jewish historian Hugh J. Schonfield, the Jewish year 33/34 AD was a Sabbatical year. The following year 34/35 was a Roman census year, when Jesus began his public ministry. According to Luke's account, he began it with verses from Isaiah:

HIS, my Lord's Spirit is upon me.
because HE has anointed me,
sent me,
to bring happiness to the humble,
to bind up the brokenhearted,
to call out to the captives: Ransom!
To the incarcerated: enlightenment!
To proclaim a year of HIS grace.

The last sentence suggests that Jesus began his public ministry with a year of jubilee. This assumption is certainly controversial, but it is shared, for example, by the theologian Yoder.

Even if the Year of Jubilee (see Exodus 25) was certainly no longer kept in Jesus' time, it can be assumed that at least in certain circles,

The "People of God" Concept

from which Jesus may have learned, corresponding time calculations were continued. It is therefore quite conceivable that the forthcoming Jubilee year (or year of remission or year of homecoming) was, among other things, legitimation and occasion for Jesus to begin his public ministry. In any case, no better prelude was conceivable for his task than the great wave of forgiveness, conversion and new beginning that was to be triggered by a jubilee year.

If it is true, as Schonfield states, that the same year was a year of the Roman census, then not only was the originally intended year of liberation perverted into a year of oppression, i.e. turned into the opposite; then also the unrest among the people and consequently the expectation of the Messiah must have been particularly great at that time.

But if we now calculate the Jubilee cycles of fifty years right up to the present, then surprisingly we not only get a coincidence with the economic Theory of Long Waves, i.e. the so-called *Kondratieff Cycle* (see also Joseph Huber, *Die verlorene Unschuld der Ökologie* [The Lost Innocence of Ecology] but we also come to the year 1934/35 and to the Sabbatical year 1933 preceding it with Hitler's seizure of power and the proclamation of the master race, i.e. a further perversion of the Jubilee conception and the People of God idea which, after all, aims at a people of service and love. Especially for us Germans this should give food for thought!

Fifty years further on we come to the year 1984/85, i.e. we live in the year 1983/84 [at the time of writing] in a Sabbatical year according to old reckoning, which is followed by a Jubilee year. In view of the international debt and the hopelessness of the international financial situation, the recommendation of the Sabbath and Jubilee verses from Deuteronomy 25 (Leviticus) seems strangely topical and compelling:

When you have celebrated the Sabbatical Year (Seven Times) and thus a total of 49 years have passed, on the tenth day of the seventh month, the Day of Atonement, you shall sound the bugle throughout the land. This is the sign that all its inhabitants will be restored to their original rights. The 50th year must be considered a year that belongs to me. It is the year of remission, when a general restoration takes place. Every Israelite who has mortgaged his inherited land will have it restored, and whoever has sold himself as a slave to another will be allowed to return to his clan.

The "People of God" Concept

In the year of remission, everyone is to get back his possession of land........

For many, this calculation with annual numbers may hardly be sufficiently justified. And yet almost the same calculation, at least with almost the same result, must have been made by the Vatican. It can hardly be a coincidence that the Pope has made 1983 a Holy Year. Why was it in 1983, of all years, that the last Holy Year was celebrated after 1950, so that the fifty-year interval from the previous one had not been observed? It can be assumed that the Vatican's decision had historical reasons, even if this was not made public.

We have observed how in history the respective due positive step was turned into the opposite by "dark powers". Thus, the year 34/35 became not the year of liberation proclaimed by Jesus but a special year of oppression by the Romans. In a much more terrible way, in the years 1933/34/35, a Sabbath and Jubilee year, the biblical idea of the departure of a people of love and service into the seizure of power was perverted by a "MASTER RACE". With the year and day of the seizure of power even something like a jubilee year of darkness was celebrated, and millions of German Christians have celebrated this witches' Sabbath together!

It can even be proved historically that some ideologists of Nazism explicitly referred to the Third Reich of Joachim von Fiore. What a challenge for insightful Germans to finally help the real Third Reich of the spirit, the Third Reich of the holy people prevail!

One can almost get goose bumps when, in our days, the dark side is once again about to take over an important concept of the people of God, to turn it into the opposite and thus to make the breakthrough of the positive more difficult or even to prevent it: For some time now, the term "autonomous" has been haunting the press as a collective term for all kinds of violent chaotic people. So if there is now a new God's people movement that strives for autonomy, there will be a great danger of lumping it together with the so-called autonomists when viewed superficially or even maliciously, just as anarchism and terrorism have long been synonymous for a superficial public.

But this should not prevent us, 1950 years after Jesus and fifty years after the seizure of power by the "master race", in view of the terrible endangerment of man and creature, to "proclaim a year of HIS grace" and to take seriously, together with like-minded people

The "People of God" Concept

all over the world, to revive the ancient idea of God's people and — expressed in non-religious terms — to form an autonomous, associative universal community of people of all races, classes, religions and world views, a worldwide autonomous network of self-governing communities, which take up the task of concretely realizing Jesus' policy of love and service, of absolute non-power and nonviolence.

Attempts of this kind have been made again and again over the past two millennia. Time and again, partial aspects of the overall concept have been realized and the torch of hope has been nurtured and passed on. Only a few of them are mentioned here:

From the monastic orders beginning with the spiritual, the Quakers and the other peace churches. The Hutterites, Oneida, Shakers, Bruderhof and all the others who have found refuge in the USA. The Moral Re-Armament Teams. From the anarchists of Spain to the soviet republic in Bavaria after WWI with Gustav Landauer. From the beginnings of the Zionists with the kibbutz movement and the contributions to it by Martin Buber, who was spiritually rooted in the Hasidism of the Jews of Eastern Europe, to the Mondcivitan Republic of Hugh J. Schonfield.

From the Findhorn community in the north of Scotland to all the other New Age communities, the communities of the emerging Aquarian Age.

Many of these attempts have strayed, failed, perished, others crippled, ossified and perverted. But they have all provided building blocks for the road to the future. The dream is still alive, and it seems that in this our time, on the one hand, the pressure of suffering is great enough, and on the other hand, through technology, science and the development of consciousness, knowledge and insight are great enough, to be able to recognize the People of God concept in its entire meaning for humanity, that is, not limited to the Judeo-Christian cultural sphere, and then to realize it on a clear basis.

What does this groundwork look like?

The members of this modern "People of God" do not represent an elite. They do not rule, they are not dominated, they are the servants of all. Like all others, they are parts of a greater whole. They realize - and in this they are an advance division - that the whole of humanity is one organism. "No one is an enemy, no one is a stranger, all are brothers and sisters, all are one". So say the Mondcivitans. Paul was on the right track when he referred to Christians as the "body of Christ". But in his conception, there were "others". However, there are no others. All are one. As long as there are others for us, we fall too easily into the temptation to build up enemy images. We cannot cope with our own problems and avoid dialogue. This leads to the fact that we permanently wage war against death and the devil within us and are constantly defeated. This situation in turn leads to the readiness to wage war against death and the devil outside of us as well. This can be observed, for example, with Luther. Friedrich Heer, the Austrian philosopher of history, comments: *The unmastered life pushes toward death and unleashes powerful energies of the will to destroy. Thereby it urgently needs scapegoats to whom it can charge the fear and the hatred, the hatred which is deeply self-hatred.* The Frenchman Girard has developed a whole theory on the subject "scapegoat", which is treated in detail by Raymund Schwager in "Do we need a scapegoat".

Jesus shows the right way: "Whoever wants to follow me, let him take up his cross. My yoke is gentle and my burden is light". "Do not resist evil, but transform evil with good".

Whoever does not wage war against evil, as Luther recommends, neither within himself nor without, but accepts it lovingly, his yoke becomes gentle, his burden becomes light. He who loves evil redeems it. Inside and outside, in the little and in the big.

And so the members of the new "people of God" do not live in the struggle against and in the separation from the "others", the evil ones, the enemies, but in an all-connectedness that includes and accepts everyone, so that at some point separation, division, and enmity may be abolished for them as well.

We have come to see our earth as a small ball in space. This wonderful blue planet, our spaceship Earth, is the home of all people, and all separation, all boundaries are unnatural. The time is ripe for Cardinal Bea's insight. He says that "the exploration of space is making people more and more aware that they form one family on this earth, and that the modern world holds untold ways and means to make humanity one family in the truest sense of the word."

This insight must be realized in an exemplary way with a clear rejection of everything that separates and a wholehearted devotion to everything that unites.

Arise, shine, for your light is coming.

Willi Haller, January 1983

Literature

Paperback series "Texte zum Nachdenken" [Texts to think about]. Herder-Verlag Freiburg

Bücher der Kündung (die Propheten des Alten Testaments) [Books of the Annunciation (the prophets of the Old Testament)] German by Martin Buber, by Jakob Hegner in Cologne

Martin Buber: Zwischen Zeit und Ewigkeit [Between Time and Eternity] by Lambert Schneider, Heidelberg

Friedrich Heer: Gottes erste Liebe [God's First Love] Bechtle-Verlag, Munich and Eßlingen

Adolf Holl: Der letzte Christ [The Last Christian], Ullstein Sachbuch 34069

Raymund Schwager: Brauchen wir einen Sündenbock [Do We Need a Scapegoat], by Kösel, Munich

Hugh J. Schonfield: The Politics of God, Texianer Verlag, Germany

Hugh J. Schonfield: The Pentecost Revolution Texianer Verlag, Germany

Joseph Huber: Die verlorene Unschuld der Ökologie [The Lost Innocence of Ecology], by S. Fischer, Frankfurt

W. Haller: The Politics of Jesus, Texianer Verlag, Germany

The Politics of Jesus

Dealing with the historical figure of Jesus of Nazareth is still a rather problematic undertaking. For some, namely devout Christians, the religious or spiritual dimension of his life and teachings is so overwhelming that general human and political aspects fade completely into the background and are usually not even perceived or even disavowed. For others, who do not know anything about the spiritual dimension, a preoccupation with this Jesus does not make much sense. What should the life of a man, an idealistic Jewish carpenter, who was executed by an occupying power almost two thousand years ago, like many others before and after him, still be of importance for us today?

And yet, studying this man is worth the effort, even if, as we choose to do today, we neglect the religious or spiritual dimension for the sake of the topic in question.

This is not so simple, however, because in the Judaism of the Bible, religion and politics were always inseparable. The great prophets were always also the great critics of the domestic and foreign policies of their time, evidently frequently the only opposition. The schizophrenic split between religion and politics has been the preserve of Christianity, which oriented religion toward the afterlife and largely shirked responsibility for this world.

For years, we Christians have been making it too easy for ourselves by granting only a religious dimension to the life and teachings of Jesus, from which consequences were to be expected in the private sphere at best. Secretly, we have smiled rather presumptuously at the undiscerning Jews of his time, believing that Jesus gave a religious-spiritual answer to a political question and challenge, whereas, as we shall see, he gave a religious and political answer to a religious and political question. However, we do not take its political dimension seriously, in the same way as his contemporaries—indeed, we refuse even to acknowledge it.

The situation at the time of Jesus

Let us try to reconstruct the situation that Jesus found himself in when he appeared with the claim, at first kept secret for understandable reasons, to be the expected Messiah. That is to say, the priestly king who would redeem Israel and who, with the redeemed Israel, the people of God, would take on the task of bringing the light to the tribes of the world in order to spread God's freedom, peace and justice "to the ends of the earth".

He encountered a political system, the Roman Empire, which in collaboration with the upper classes of the country had imposed its principles: power, domination, violence, coercion, exploitation, oppression, to name but a few terms that characterized imperialism then as now.

These are principles which, point by point, represent the exact opposite of what the Jewish traditions had transmitted as the ideal of a reign of God and a society free of human rule, an ideal which had coined the terms freedom, mercy, justice, peace, and which, following Hugh J. Schonfield, I would like to call messianism, the opposite of imperialism.

The challenge Jesus faced was not to cast out the devil with Beelzebub—that was what the Zealots were aiming at—that is, to fight imperialism with imperialism, but to show a way how imperialism could be overcome and messianism could take its place. Jesus faced this challenge and obviously, building on the traditions of his people, found an answer that is not only valid then and there but also today and here and everywhere in the world and is probably the only way to fulfill step by step the first request of Jesus in the Lord's Prayer, "Thy kingdom come", to soften the dominance of imperialistic principles in our world (starting with our hearts) and to come closer to the great utopia of a domination-free community of all people and all creatures on this earth.

Jesus saw through the dangers of power. He resisted the temptation, "I will give you dominion over all these kingdoms in all their greatness and beauty", and formulated and lived a policy not only of non-violence but also of conscious powerlessness. The extent to which he confronted and dealt with the political reality of his time can be seen in the following quotes attributed to him:

Whoever strikes you on the right cheek, turn to him the other also; and whoever wants to start a dispute with you and take your skirt, let him have your coat as well; and whoever forces you to go one mile, go with him two.

Three images with the same answer that gains central meaning through multiple repetition: Do not resist evil, but transform evil by good. The one affected bows to the constraint, but not grudgingly, swallowing the anger. He recognizes in the other a brother who goes astray, who loses his own dignity by violating the dignity of the oppressed. This was particularly clear in the last image, which was concretely related to an everyday situation of the time, and which, unfortunately, in modern translations has been created by the loss of historical reference:

The Jewish people were called upon by the occupying power to perform services. One of these services consisted of requiring each member of the occupying power to carry his luggage for a distance of one mile. It was certainly heavily discussed among the freedom-loving Jews how one should face this demand. Jesus gives an answer, provocative until today: neither violent nor non-violent resistance is recommended, but the apparent yet active and positive submission purposefully and positively through the voluntary second step beyond the acceptance of the affront. The first mile is enforced by the oppressor and makes the other the oppressed. The second mile should be the understanding and forgiving gift of a free man to a free man.

I wonder where and how we could turn the other cheek and go the second mile on the issue of so-called rearmament.

Also the harmless, because soft and gentle sounding sentence from the so-called Sermon on the Mount,

> *Blessed are the meek*
> *for they shall inherit the earth.*

It was perhaps rather a clear answer to the question, which probably came mainly from the Zealots, whether the Romans would "possess the earth" forever, or in which way the oppression could be put to an end. A clear rejection of the proponents of violence, but probably also of all claims to power, dominion and possession. For he probably meant, "The earth will be entrusted to those who have not aspired to it".

Indifference to power

The number of those from the Judeo-Christian tradition who derive a justification for violence and the threat of violence is decreasing, even if the mainstream churches, as can be seen from the question of the arms race, still find it difficult to clearly represent a Jesuanic policy. So on the question of violence, the clouds are clearing. But we are still strangely indifferent to power, although power is the mother of violence. For example, Prof. Dr. Theodor Ebert, one of the great advocates of nonviolence, writes in issue 4/83 of *wub*: "A nice success, however, is that most groups in the peace and ecology movements have understood that nonviolent action is an extraordinary set of instruments. with which power can be developed." In the same issue, Dietmar Böhm writes: "For example, this very question: 'How do I, as a Christian, stand with weapons of mass destruction?' should play a decisive role in the December church council elections in Württemberg. Here we can practise a return to life by voting only for candidates who say NO to all weapons of mass destruction. Making this election also a vote for life would mean the consistent continuation of the *Kirchentag* (Church Congress) motto."

We are thoughtlessly pouring new wine into old wineskins. We do not understand that the desired conversion to life cannot be achieved by way of seizing power, even if this path is started in modest guise in the parish councils!

Jesus also creates clear conditions with regard to the question of power. This was not only at the beginning of his ministry, but was also his central message. Light and salt need neither the power of the dictator nor the power of the democratic majority—on the contrary: too much light would be unbearable, too much salt unpalatable. Jesus turns this realist, deplorable insight of the Old Testament, that only a minority, a remnant, is capable of conversion, on its head: only a minority is needed, but it must be on fire, ready to surrender. And yet we think we can spare ourselves this by fighting for power and majorities.

Finally, the question of power is also the central theme on the last evening with his disciples. His statements on this point are underlined by the symbolic action of the washing of feet, which, as Peter's reaction shows, was unheard of in terms of difference in status. The importance of the statements is thus emphatically underlined. They acquire the character of a legacy of decisive importance, a legacy that straightforwardly creates a link between the great story of temptation at the beginning and the cross at the end of his ministry. The life and teaching of Jesus cannot be seen otherwise than as a clear rejection of any quest for power even and especially in the field of politics. Let us look again at the last evening with his disciples in response: Matthew omits the washing of feet and the statements belonging to it. Perhaps he did not know anything about it: perhaps it does not fit enough into his picture of Jesus as the King, that is already depicted in his birthday story and that culminates in the Sermon on the Mount, where he depicts Jesus as the second Moses, who gives the new covenant its basic law, that is, a new constitution to the people of God.

Mark does not know anything about it either, but Luke writes: "The kings of the world oppress their peoples, and the tyrants let themselves be called "benefactors of the people". With you it must be different. The highest among you must be like the lowest, and the leader like the servant."

John begins with the washing of feet and has Jesus say, "I am your Lord and Teacher, and yet I have just washed your feet. From now on, you are to wash one another's feet. I have given you an example so that you also may act as I have acted towards you. I tell you, a servant is not greater than his master."

How does he come to this rigorous rejection of power. How is the world to be changed with complete powerlessness, how is the people of God without power to fulfill its task of being a light to the peoples of the world, that my freedom may reach to the edge of the world?

Jesus knows, as we should all know today, that real change cannot be achieved through the pursuit of power and majorities, at least not sustainable change. Pressure creates counter-pressure, and with every change of power, the reaction is only waiting for the next change of power and majorities, because no change of hearts has taken place. And those who, even with the best of intentions, want to get into power and perhaps eventually do, eventually corrupt themselves.

Isn't that a bit overstated? Aren't there also quite benevolent rulers where neither the leaders nor the led are "enslaved"?

Dialogical principle according to Buber

The problem of the question of power can perhaps be best illustrated by Martin Buber's dialogical principle. This principle says in broad outline that man is designed for the Thou, indeed that he needs dialogue to become human. The encounter with the Thou takes place when I perceive and accept the other in his otherness as an equal subject standing before me. But if I accept the other in his being different and resist the temptation to "convince him by all means" of the correctness of my conviction, if I adhere with Rabbi Nachman to letting the other go his own way in freedom on the path of service, just as God gives us the freedom to go our own way, then often enormous tensions arise from different perceptions, which become perceptible as pain and suffering. Our aversion to pain now tempts us to break off the dialogue (or not to seek it at all) and to impose our conviction on the other person by all means—in political life even to the point of physical annihilation.

We are trying to gain the upper hand. To have the majority and the power to impose our ideas without the laborious and lengthy and painful process of dialogue. This leads, however, to the fact that the one who thinks differently loses his status as "Thou" and becomes the "It", the object, which becomes alienated when I gain the upper hand. Collectively, oligarchies, parties and factions emerge. Dialogue becomes limited to the faction, the group of like-minded people, within which there is no tension that could become fruitful. Between the factions (or parties), only monologues take place. Showcase speeches are given; dialogue is absent; the process of becoming human is blocked. But since the human being is designed for dialogue, its absence is felt as a deficiency, even if mostly unconsciously. Attempts are then made to compensate for this lack by gaining power (here lies the addictive character of which Burkhardt speaks), whereby the number of people within a faction with whom dialogue is conducted and endured also becomes smaller and smaller. In the extreme case—most clearly visible in the example of Stalin—it comes to complete isolation and loneliness with persecution mania as a bonus.

Any lasting change is therefore only possible through an unconditional willingness to engage in dialogue, that is, through surrender, as Jesus' examples of the light that consumes and the salt that dissolves clearly show. Overcoming the aversion to pain and accepting suffering as the only way to make the tension arising from opposites fruitful is clearly expressed by Jesus and, and also, in more recent times, unequivocally formulated by Gandhi.

Every attempt to achieve something by way of power, whether by parliamentary means from the parish council up to the national parliament or through the extra-parliamentary mobilization of masses, in the peace movement or elsewhere, is therefore a perfectly legitimate attempt at change, but it has nothing to do with Jesusanic politics and the attempt to follow Jesus. In the way of power, the one who thinks differently is excluded, turned into an opponent. One joins together against him in as increasing a number as possible. With Jesus, the one who thinks differently is included, perceived, accepted, even if he abuses his power. He becomes the neighbor for whom I am jointly responsible.

Starting with self-commitment

The Jesuanic way proceeds through self-commitment and begins with the effort to "remove the beam from one's own eye". Martin Buber says: The Archimedean point for changing the world is changing oneself.

This path begins with self-commitment and returns again and again to self-commitment, since the failure to change means that we have still not sufficiently become salt and light, otherwise there would have to be light in the darkness. Surely this was also the tragedy of Jesus and his inner anguish. He had to witness the fact that the conversion he had preached was not being accomplished, and thus saw the great catastrophe approaching.

He wept over Jerusalem because he realized that the downfall of the city had become inevitable. People, then as now, were not ready to give up the way of power and violence and seek the way of love and service. Even his sacrificial death did not trigger conversion, then as now. Already a few decades after his death there was the great uprising that ended with the destruction of Jerusalem and the annihilation of most of the population. Since then, too, violence has been done to man and nature countless times, often even explicitly in his name.

Looking at it superficially and politically, his death was only the last consequence of his life and his teachings, a death that placed him in the ranks of the great failures, who nevertheless changed the world more than all the successful ones, because over the centuries they had shown and walked paths that nourished the hope for a better future.

The messianic task has yet to be fulfilled

The even greater tragedy of his life and its significance for the development of humanity lies in the fact that his main goal, to set God's people on the path of fulfilling their messianic task for all mankind, has remained rudimentary. Then as now, the peoples of this world, our nation-states, can only find their way out of their hopeless aberration in the undergrowth of imperialism, at least for those who take the Judeo-Christian tradition of the Bible seriously, if the people of God, or in non-religious terms, an autonomous, associative universal community of people, concretely exemplifies to them the realization of Jesus' politics.

It is about this concrete exemplary life, individually and collectively. This is what the images of salt and light, of the city on the mountain mean. And it is an example worthy of imitation that, in messianism, takes the place of the solitary decisions of the strong men of politics or of the majority decisions of the rulers in imperialism as the bearer and trigger of change. The majority decision allows only the subjugation of the minority; example, on the other hand, opens the way for everyone to decide, in freedom and with respect for his own dignity, for or against following it. This freedom is one of the central concerns of the Bible.

It is therefore a matter of putting Jesus' policy into practice step by step, both on a small and a large scale, individually and collectively. We do not need to wait for miracles to do this. The task is within our grasp, and no one and nothing but our own lethargy prevents us from getting started.

Literature:

Hugh J. Schonfield: The Politics of God, Texianer Verlag, Tuningen

Martin Buber Das Dialogische Prinzip Lambert Schneider, Heidelberg

Dualism and polarity

These two terms may be unfamiliar to most people, but behind them lies a conflict that not only goes back to the dawn of mankind and has religious roots, but also strongly influences our lives to this day. For example, when U.S. President George W. Bush Jr. refers to certain Asian countries as the "axis of evil", he reveals a dualistic way of thinking that seems to be widespread in the U.S. and obviously characterizes fundamentalism regardless of ideology.

Both terms have a common starting point. They are rooted in opposites that are recognizable to all of us and are called good and evil, light and dark, day and night, and so on. But then come the crucial differences. Dualism sees these opposites as irreconcilable, fighting each other with the goal of mutual annihilation. Whereas when thinking in polarities, these opposites remain indissolubly connected to each other for the earthly existence of the human race. It is about the "shadow integration", as the great Swiss psychologist C. G. Jung called it. One of the great minds of the Middle Ages, Nicholas of Cues, spoke of the coincidence of these opposites, however, only in the infinite, in the divine; speaking of the COINCIDENTIA OPPOSITORUM. According to this, our earthly existence is characterized by opposites, and it is futile to try to destroy the darkness in this world. Even the ancient Greeks knew that attempting to slay the "dragon" is in vain. For every head cut off—according to their mythology—the Hydra grows eight new ones.

The Christian Church has always fought dualism, from Gnosticism to the Manichaeans and the Cathars, who were killed and exterminated in what was probably the first genocide in European history. Its great spirits, from St. Hildegard of Bingen to the aforementioned Cusan, urged it to be overcome. And yet she fared as she had to fare. She tried to annihilate her "darkness" and fell prey to it, namely to dualism. In its wake, Western thinking became dualistic, right to this day—even if it pretends to be completely non-church and non-religious. It was not until Depth Psychology, coined or at least influenced by C. G. Jung, went new ways and began to think and act in polarities, i.e. in the indissoluble connection and interaction of opposites. This learning step is still pending for all Christian churches and for Western thinking in general.

Might and Power

"You will not succeed by human might and power, but by my Spirit". Thus says the fourth chapter of the Old Testament book of Zechariah in the Bible. And yet, in the Judeo-Christian tradition that attitude has shaped the entire Occident, religious or otherwise. The exercise of power and violence is still considered to this day to be a basic prerequisite for the reasonably peaceful coexistence of national and international society. There is no doubt that Jesus himself and the so-called early church, i.e. early Christianity, fundamentally rejected the use of military force, and consequently military service of any kind was out of the question for a Christian of that time. Power and violence in other forms were also considered highly problematic. This has all changed considerably, and even for the radical Christian it seems impossible to completely renounce power and violence, even if it is only towards the "underage", i.e. children and all those who at least temporarily may behave as "dependent". At the same time, it must remain open who counts as such and when. In most cases, the "powerful" determine who counts as a "minor" and thus is not a subject, but becomes an object of their (usually quite benevolent) manipulation.

It appears necessary to define these terms clearly, or at least to establish their meaning for our consideration, before any further consideration of them makes sense. The great German sociologist Max Weber has pointed us in the right direction when he defines power as the ability to enforce one's will even against the will of others. If necessary by force—would have to be added, because usually the rulers have at their disposal, either directly or indirectly, the necessary means of open or structural violence to enforce their own will. According to Martin Buber, the Thou thus becomes the It, the subject becomes the object.

We are unfortunately not dealing with unambiguous black-and-white areas in relation to these two concepts and the behaviors associated with them as we would like to do. It must therefore ultimately be left to the conscience of the individual to draw personal boundaries within which power and violence are indispensable and outside which rejection and refusal must be equally indispensable. In this context, it is quite conceivable that the individual may apply more radical standards to himself than to others. It is important to know that—in spite of the radical attitude of Jesus and the early Christians—everyone would like to possess as much power as possible and, if necessary, would use violence to enforce it. That power and violence possess addictive qualities and threaten to corrupt character is unknown to most. Lord Acton, for example, said that power corrupts, and absolute power corrupts absolutely. To prevent this, power is indeed transferred (ranging from associations to the state), but it is controlled (for example, by regular meetings of the members or, say, of the parliament), and its exercise is usually limited in time (for example, for the duration of the term of office). Of course, there are exceptions to this. They usually involve money and assets.

Two particularly sensitive areas of the exercise of power and force are repeatedly the subject of public debate. One area relates to the state's monopoly on the use of force, which means that only the state, and not the citizen, is granted the right to enforce the fulfillment of its duties by force if necessary. The police in its various forms and border protection serve this purpose. In principle, this area is virtually unquestioned; the only controversy is over how far the powers of the state and the police may go. The spectrum is broad: from a civil state to a police state. That is what is being argued about today and will certainly continue to be argued about in the future. More problematic is the area covered by the Armed Forces in our country. Originally, the German Armed Forces' mission within NATO was limited to the ability and readiness to defend Western Europe. Today, that no longer applies. It seems highly doubtful, however, whether its deployment in Afghanistan can be justified, even within the coalition parties of the government.

Companies are always striving to increase their power, especially through centralized mergers, which often manifest themselves as megalomania. A prime example of this is Daimler-Benz, which has not only joined forces with Chrysler but has also cast a greedy eye on Mitsubishi. One could pass over this with a bitter smile if it were not for the fact that more and more of the small stores in the inner cities were disappearing, and that in the banking industry, too, the small borrower is increasingly losing his trusted partner.

Money, Community and Property

Without a doubt, money is one of mankind's greatest inventions. Without money as a medium of exchange, it would be impossible to imagine a society based on the division of labor as it is today throughout the world. But its role as a medium of exchange does not adequately describe its tasks. The second function of money, which is in principle just as important, is based on the fact that it can be easily saved, that capital can be accumulated with monetary assets. This saving and the associated renunciation of consumption may be problematic for some advocates of unlimited growth, but they are indispensable because so many projects cannot be financed from current income and very often require the cooperation of many people to finance them.

The necessary criticism of our financial behavior is therefore not directed against money per se, but against the way in which we deal with savings capital, to whom we make it available and with what conditions this is connected. The pure doctrine proclaims that money is not a commodity, is based on trust and involves obligations, and therefore cannot possibly entitle it to multiplication, i.e. interest. This is quite true, especially since most monetary currencies are no longer backed by gold, and their value is guaranteed virtually exclusively by trust.

The problem arises when it comes to interest, both in principle and in the way in which the interest rate is set. The fundamental critique rejects interest outright. The criticism is based on the Bible (which rejects the taking of interest from fellow citizens) and the Koran (which takes the same line as the Bible). As is well known, Jesus goes even further than the so-called Old Testament. He says quite simply: lend without expecting anything back. The pros and cons of taking interest could be argued. The fact is that it has a downright murderous offspring, namely compound interest. This ensures that in the absence of servicing debt or in the case of persistent abstention from consumption, exponential growth will occur, i.e. an explosive increase in money. If, for example, a baby was given a federal treasury bond worth ten thousand marks as a gift in its cradle a few years ago, its value will accumulate to about one million marks by the time this person reaches retirement age if he or she refrains from consuming it. The great debt crisis of the so-called Third World has its roots here.

In the face of this plight, (compare this with Silvio Gesell, the doyen of interest-free or negative interest rates in more recent times), to demand a complete renunciation of interest payments misses the realities. It is not only that billions of dollars are lent every day by all sorts of banks and private individuals, and explicitly linked to the condition of paying interest on it. Moreover, almost everyone claims an annual increase for their monetary assets that goes beyond compensation for inflation.

Our sense of realism demands this, and the zeitgeist seems to agree.

Regrettably, it is usually overlooked that our attitude on the question of interest rates is related to an isolatedness and individualization, which we all demand and promote, and which seeks to achieve the greatest possible financial security, especially for our old age. To forego this protection presupposes a community of solidarity that would truly be worthy of the name. Unfortunately, today this is virtually non-existent.

Much more problematic is the way in which interest rates are set, as is practiced almost everywhere today. It is based on the so-called "credit rating" and ranges from AAA 1 for the best, most creditworthy addresses down to credit seekers who are not creditworthy at all and who are therefore not granted any loans. It is lowest for AAA 1 addresses and grows on the way down, so that in the end, in effect, those who need the credit most pay the highest interest rates, and vice versa. The old phrase is confirmed: Those who do not need money may borrow any amount, at the lowest interest rates, and those who need it most will receive none.

One last point needs to be mentioned in connection with money. We have an almost holy awe for everything connected with it. Not only do we rarely or never talk about it, it is also virtually untaxed. It is true that there is an insurance tax, but otherwise the entire monetary system is tax-free, while all transactions involving goods or other services are subject to sales tax or value-added tax. It seems urgent to impose a sales tax of at least 0.1% on all stock exchange transactions and, moreover, on all bank transactions.

This would not only open up an enormous source of revenue for the states, but would also reduce the number of speculative transactions, which are a fire hazard everywhere.

In the whole discussion about money and capital, it is usually overlooked that the capital input per workplace has grown enormously in recent decades. According to figures from the Federal Statistical Office in Wiesbaden, we now need an average of around a quarter of a million deutsche marks (or roughly half that in euros) to finance a job with all the trimmings. As a rule, employees do not have sufficient financial assets (or corresponding creditworthiness) to raise this amount. Outside investors are therefore indispensable. And how are they to be paid or remunerated?

And now to the question of ownership. Here, too, there are no simple black and white answers.

Property as we know it today probably came into being in the first half of the last pre-Christian millennium. Before that, everything belonged to everyone, i.e. it was common property; private property was largely unknown. This changed with the tremendous upheavals of that time, which were probably mainly due to climatic conditions.

Thus the private ownership of land came into being. Among the ancient Germanic peoples, for example, private ownership of land was largely unknown. There was the commons, the parish common and the fief. That seemed to be sufficient for the most part. For Westerners today, it is virtually a sacred cow that must be defended at all costs. A differentiated approach seems to be called for in this context.

No one seems to seriously question private ownership for the objects of everyday use. With house ownership this changes, and with land ownership even more so. Ownership of a residential building seems to play the role of an additional kind of skin for Westerners. Private ownership in the case of house ownership is therefore probably morally unobjectionable, even if ownership, for example, in foundation hands and a lifelong right of residence would seem to make more sense. It becomes problematic only if the house property exceeds one's own needs, thus mostly financial investment (and tax saving). A similar situation applies to the ownership of land.

No one will even seriously question ownership of operating assets for the founder and initial business owner. Here too — as with many questions of ownership—it only becomes problematic for the first or second subsequent generation, because they have contributed and continue to contribute little or nothing to the creation and preservation of the assets.

There is no doubt that ownership of more or less large amounts of money that are not used to cover one's own living costs is the most problematic. It serves only to increase and exercise power, which is generally not very well qualified for this purpose and is of little use to the debtor and the general public. Often enough, it even harms them. The ideal here would undoubtedly be to place the sums exceeding one's own monetary needs in a foundation and use them to cover part of the capital needs of the economy and the rest of society. The key word here is "neutralization of capital".

Unemployment

There are two things that usually get short shrift in our public discussion.

The first is the fact that economic growth alone (highly problematic in itself) cannot solve the problem of persistent mass unemployment, and — linked to this — that employment figures in industry (the secondary sector) are likely to continue to decline.

For example, in the automotive industry, the rule of thumb is that output (ultimately expressed in terms of the number of vehicles delivered) per employee hour should be doubled every ten years or so. In terms of the number of employees, this means that if the number of hours worked and the number of vehicles delivered remain the same, the number of employees will be halved over this period and unemployment in this sector will double. The same is essentially true for most other industries.

The so-called three-sector theory is based on the dramatic decline in employment in the primary sector (which in our case is mainly agriculture) and the secondary sector (which is mainly industry). This decline applies to every industrialized country and can be seen in the official statistics. In Germany, for example, in the second half of the nineteenth century more than half of all workers were employed in agriculture; today the figure is less than three percent. In the first half of the twentieth century, the same was true for industry; today, less than one-third of all employed persons work in industry. Quite obviously, the tertiary sector (the service sector) is not able to compensate for the employment losses in the primary and secondary sectors.

A number of steps seem indispensable to do justice to this, and they will be outlined briefly here.

On the one hand, women's employment has risen dramatically in recent decades. There has been no corresponding decline in men's employment. It seems that men have not noticed this development, neither as employers nor as employees. At any rate, they have not drawn any conclusions from it.

Secondly, classical, highly capital-intensive gainful employment must be complemented by more labor-intensive gainful employment, such as that demanded and promoted by E. F. Schumacher with his "Appropriate Technology". Even people who do not (or no longer) belong to the so-called high-performance elite or who are simply among the more fortunate have a right to earn their living through their own work and not to be kept barely alive by state funding.

Third, it is inevitable that social security contributions will no longer be levied and financed exclusively from income from gainful employment. This has abstruse consequences (for example, the company that lays off employees is rewarded in terms of tax policy, and the company that hires is punished accordingly); it also encourages undeclared work, as the state government in Baden-Württemberg already noted in 1982 in a study on economic development.

There are therefore a number of steps to be taken if we are really serious about tackling this problem. The first of these seems to be to create the necessary awareness.

Flexible Working Hours

Flexible working hours do not automatically create new jobs. Usually, the opposite is the case. After all, flexible working hours bring about the optimum use of available personnel capacity and, associated with this, the avoidance of idle time as well as the avoidance of a lot of overtime. New jobs are only created when flexible working hours are used to decouple (usually expand) the operating or functional time of the workplace from the (net) working time actually worked by employees and when this results in multiple staffing. However, the new jobs created are usually at the expense of others because they increase the performance and competitiveness of the workplace. Even though flexible working hours tend to be viewed negatively in terms of employment policy, the advantages make their introduction advisable almost everywhere. In the age of the service industry, with its emphasis on work on demand, it is becoming a matter of course for everyone. This applies both to its duration (i.e., full- and part-time work) and to its distribution.

There are two different focal points to flexible working hours. Each of these can stand alone, but they can also be linked together.

In the case of one element, the amount of working time worked per working period (e.g. per week) is variable. It deviates from the standard (approximately 35 hours per week) upwards and downwards by an agreed amount (in the example, approximately plus/minus five hours per week, i.e. from 30 to 40 hours per week).

The other focus is on the decoupling of operating or functional time from the (net) working time actually worked, as already mentioned above. It is initially irrelevant whether this is done in the traditional way or whether it is simply a matter of compensating for the fact that net working time is only 75 to 85% of gross working time. After all, every employee has four to six weeks of annual vacation and is sick for an average of two weeks a year. In any case, there will be more or less rigidly organized multiple staffing.

The introduction of time accounts for all employees is indispensable in both cases. In this context, it is necessary to examine whether one time account per employee is sufficient, which would have to be kept in the manner similar to a checking account at the bank, how high the so-called time balance may be allowed to grow upwards and downwards, i.e. which limits appear appropriate, whether several time accounts should be introduced per employee, for example a time account in the form of a checking account for the time balance and a time account in the form of a savings account for saving long-term leave up to and including a sabbatical year, or even a multi-level time account, namely a so-called traffic light account, with several levels of disposal rights.

How flexible working hours can be designed in a humane way is a completely different question and requires detailed investigation and agreement.

All of this requires clarification and mutual agreement and must ultimately lead to a company agreement or organizational instruction if abuse and chaos are to be avoided.

The Human Job

In a recent article entitled, "The Job Blahs: Who wants to work?" published by the American magazine Newsweek, reference was made to a report which indicated that nearly half of the American workers are dissatisfied with their jobs and suggested that something had better be done to make work more attractive, interesting and meaningful. According to this report, the work force in America is changing with more and more workers growing restless because of "dull, repetitive, seemingly meaningless tasks, offering little challenge or autonomy". In their book, "Where have all the robots gone", cited in the same article, scientists Sheppard and Herrick reported an in-depth study of 400 male union workers and concluded that one-third of them — particularly the young ones — were alienated from their jobs and could not be assuaged with the typical rewards of more money, shorter hours or longer vacations. They went on to assert, "Worker dissatisfaction metamorphosed from a hobby horse of the "tender minded" to a fire-breathing dragon because workers began to translate their feelings of dissatisfaction into alienated behavior. Turnover rates are climbing. Absenteeism has increased as much as 100% in the past ten years in the automobile industry. Workers talk back to their bosses. They no longer accept the authoritarian way of doing things".

There can be little doubt that this report reflects the situation not only of the United States but of any highly industrialized country, even if the degree of just how serious the problems are may vary from country to country. More and more often strikes, high, employee turnover and absenteeism not only reflect problems of poor pay but of unsatisfactory working conditions and poor management-labour relations, anywhere in the western world.

This is of course alarming news not only for any company boss who realizes the importance of the economical well-being of any society. The question is only "what is being done about it?"

Under the headline "job enrichment" all sorts of programs and plans are being worked out and tried, all designed to make the employee happier and more satisfied with what he is doing. Some no doubt will be doomed and some will succeed but the basic attitude with which employee and management approach the problem will most probably make all the difference.

Wherever the employee is still looked upon as a living piece of equipment usable and disposable as the situation requires, a job enrichment program obviously is nothing more than better fodder and a more beautiful cage for the beast. But the beast no doubt, will take little time to realize this. The worker realizing he is still being used, still manipulated, still nothing more than a cost factor - like materials and equipment, will soon resume being bored, frustrated and rebellious.

Unless management realizes that the total work force is a community of human beings and not a number of employees who accept a job for a certain price which is primarily determined by the weight (the power) they can bring to bear at the bargaining table - any program to solve the problems will only scratch the surface.

AUTHORITARIAN MANAGEMENT HAS NO FUTURE.

THE OLD HIERARCHY PYRAMID MUST GO.

Cooperative management with little or no

hierarchy will take over with the manager being the servant of the organization rather than its master. New forms of organization will have to emerge, fluid rather than rigidly structured with the formation of mostly self-administrating teams and groups as the major functional bodies of the future. Employee participation in decision-making, profits and even capital will become a must. The workable limits of all these concepts must of course be calculated. It would, for example, be stupid to ask the operator of a lathe to participate in the decision on whether or not to use a computer in the bookkeeping department or to enter the South African market, but he must be asked if a new lathe should be bought or whether the workshop he works in should be reshaped.

Who is going to work this all out? The problems are pressing and most of the answers exist only in theory.

Unfortunately the unions from their historical role still put and quite often have to put their emphasis only on higher pay and additional material benefits. They have however, largely failed to use their funds to create model enterprises, demonstrating how these problems can be solved without losing economic viability. Too often, when they appear as employers, they behave as much like old-fashioned capitalists as any of their adversaries!

The employers on the other hand still consider highest possible profits their basic aim, an attitude which forces them to spend as little as possible on payroll and improved working conditions to get the highest possible output. Since personnel is primarily a cost factor, the question of social responsibility hardly comes up and the complex mixture of needs and abilities of the employee finds only lopsided consideration. The yardstick of input and output in terms of cash, certainly is a very crude tool to measure what is happening in our offices and factories.

Some might suggest that these problems are primarily problems of the capitalistic Western society. However, anybody with some knowledge of the situation in the Communist East knows only too well that the lot of the average worker in the East is certainly no more attractive than the lot of his colleague in the West. The stifling hand of the bureaucratic establishment of the state-run economies of the East leaves little or no room for freedom and self-determination for the worker and his economic situation is not very favorable either. The implications of what we propose are, however, reaching further than the area which is covered by our quest for humanization of work.

As Ota Sik, Czechoslovakia's most eminent economist (in exile) recently pointed out, "the inflationary spiral is the product of three developments which have taken place since the last war. The labour market has grown tight and the trade unions extremely powerful, which has resulted in rapidly growing wages. At the same time, consumption grew apace, thus encouraging price increases. And finally, the governments have been under increasing pressure for more and more services, so that taxes had to go up." One of the most important steps to solve the problem, in Sik's view is "to give the workers a share in the profits and in the decision-making process of their enterprises, so that they lose their present obsession with ever-increasing wages...".

No doubt, Sik is right. To break the inflationary spiral, the emphasis has to shift from wage increases to profit sharing. If an employee can bank on substantial income through profit sharing the basic wage loses its overwhelming and overall importance.

And if both labour and management learn

The Human Job

to cooperate as partners and work together for a common goal rather than fight each other, a motivational surge can flow through the companies and the economy, producing much better results than hitherto. There are quite a number of encouraging tests and experiments going on in various fields but what we are lacking is a concentrated effort to solve these problems in the largest possible context. Here is our challenge.

A lot of work has to be done, both in theory and even more in experimental practice. But the outlines of the new structures are already visible at least for those who try to look into the future with an effort to humanize work to make our offices and factories more liveable places, without losing their economic viability. Places where the dignity of man is being restored, where he is trusted and not policed and where opportunities are offered to grow and accept responsibility. The concept of flexible working hours which free the worker from the tyranny of the clock has proved by its success that trust is honored and responsibility, if delegated properly, is readily accepted and competently handled. This is a hopeful sign and encourages us to continue on the road outlined herein.

From *The Mondcivitan Bridge* 1974

Solidarity — the Price of Future Employment

The enormous technological achievements of recent years, which we can expect to continue, have to a great extent led to improvements in productivity which cannot be matched by a comparable growth in consumption. This must result in unemployment — at least until we learn to practise true solidarity.

In the midst of the oil crisis of the seventies the experts were still claiming that the provision of services, the so-called tertiary sector, was the growth-point of the future. They said it could take on all the manpower made redundant by mechanization and automation in the manufacturing industry, the secondary sector[1]. The politicians eagerly

1 The four sectors of employment:
   Agriculture, the primary sector;
   Industry, the secondary sector;
   Services, the tertiary sector;
   The quaternary sector which includes the self-employed

echoed this idea and repeated it with superficial optimism until recently.

The facts tell a different story. The decrease in the number of jobs in the secondary sector has continued as expected. But at the same time a wave of rationalization has broken over the tertiary sector. The introduction of modern electronics, above all computers, in banks, insurance companies, postal services, railways, is making ever increasing numbers redundant. This development has yet to run its full course.

What can be done? First, it is crucial that we reach a consensus in assessing the situation. We shall remain at the mercy of these trends until we accept 'that the economic system is no longer in a position to guarantee full employment', to quote Professor Nobutane Kiuchi of Japan.

When the total work available decreases while the number of employees or those seeking work remains the same (or, as at present, increases), unemployment can only be reduced if the work available is distributed differently. A reduction in working hours per person therefore seems obvious.

For various reasons, there are problems

and do-it-yourself.

about reducing the length of the working life, although it can be a significant help in combating unemployment. Similarly, if the working week were cut substantially, that would help. But recent French experience shows that a reduction of one hour per week for nearly everyone leads to few appointments — employers used every possible means to keep up production with reduced manpower. Something less marginal is needed.

Suppose, for example, that in West Germany at the moment an annual wage increase of about five per cent is acceptable. A two-year wage agreement would mean a total increase of about ten per cent. It should be possible, out of solidarity with the unemployed, to reach an agreement to take this increase in the form of reduced working hours. In this way a 40-hour week would be reduced at a stroke to 36 hours. If the 36-hour week were introduced in the middle of the lifespan of a two-year wage agreement, the employer would have a year to prepare for the changes in organization. The cost of transition would be fairly divided — in the first year the employer enjoys the advantage (same hours worked, no wage increase) but in the second year he would have to pay out the same wage for ten per cent less work.

For a company not working at full capacity the two-year pause in the wage bill would give an important breather; they would not suffer from the reduced personnel capacity as they would not be using it anyway. Companies working to full capacity would have to take on more people. The 36-hour week would have advantages, too. It could be divided into four days, or, with three employees doing two jobs, a six-day week of 54 hours would be possible. This would mean improved use of working resources.

Will we reach the consensus to take such a courageous step?

We should start by discussing whether it is morally justifiable in the face of mounting unemployment to continue to maintain that the stresses of overtime, shiftwork and nightwork are 'compensated' by the boost they give to our income. The psychological and physical harm they may do cannot be repaired by money. And the cost of any illness or disability they cause must be borne by society.

In this situation the trade unions ought to support a wages policy which pays for overtime, shiftwork, unsocial hours or unpleasant work not in extra cash but in time off.

Investigations by the German Ministry of Labour and Social Welfare into overtime and bonuses indicate that if these payments were systematically converted from money to time off, several hundred thousand more people would find employment. This would surely be worthwhile.

To examine possible future trends we need to look at developments so far. In agriculture, the primary sector, working hours depend on the weather and the season, and vary in length. The secondary sector, industrial production, created its own peculiar method of organizing work—standard hours under fixed conditions. This was understandable. It was modelled on monasteries, workhouses and the army. Mental laziness and a tendency towards authoritarian thinking led the tertiary sector to model its working hours on those of the secondary. It was therefore overlooked for a long time that the demands on the two sectors differ considerably.

In the secondary sector variations in the volume of work while manpower capacity remains unchanged (as it does when working hours are constant) can be compensated within certain limits by varying delivery periods and stock levels. But in the tertiary sector such variations immediately affect the full use of manpower. A telephonist, for example, cannot deal on Monday afternoon with a call which will come on Tuesday. Nor can a shop assistant make a sale in advance (build up stocks) or keep a customer waiting in the shop unduly (include a delivery period).

So it would not be extraordinary if the tertiary sector got over its mindless copying of the secondary and found the pattern of work to which it is best suited. This is a varying pattern of flexible working hours.

Has the development of new patterns of work gone as far as it can for the moment? Not at all. Greater freedom in the distribution of working hours by such means as flexitime is not the end point. There are many indications that a further step is already emerging.

Many people, at least during part of their lives, are not interested in a permanent, full-time job and are therefore looking for temporary employment. The quaternary sector, those working for themselves and those in occupations not geared to gaining reward, is growing in importance. The do- it-yourself movement provides evidence of this, as does the increasing turnover in craft, hobby and woodwork markets. This sector also includes housewives, gardening enthusiasts and those practising various forms of self-sufficiency. The unemployed also belong to it, although unwillingly. They are mostly occupied in activities which bring no financial reward, unless they are taking part in the black economy.

The signs are that the quaternary sector is growing in importance and that we are approaching the moment when it will replace the tertiary as the dominant one. This is signalled by such slogans as 'the leisured society' or 'postindustrial society'.

It is highly likely that a dominant quaternary sector will lead to new work patterns — just as the tertiary has done. The quaternary sector will see 'individual working hours', whereby not only the distribution but also the number of hours worked in a week, or a year, can to some extent be determined by the employee himself. He will be able to change them again and again during his working life. This concept of 'individual working hours' includes such work patterns as progressive entry into gainful employment (e.g. part-time training), prolonged leave of absence (sabbaticals), job-sharing, gradual retirement and voluntary reduction in working hours to help combat unemployment.

When the German Institute of Labour looked at people's preferences in working hours, the surprising result was that more than half of those in full-time jobs said they were ready in principle to work and earn less. It remains to be seen how many of them will go through with this when it comes to the crunch.

Some teachers in the English Midlands show that it can happen. They are given the chance to work full-time for four years and have the fifth one free, drawing 80 per cent of the full salary throughout. This means that for every four participants one unemployed teacher can be appointed. The total expenditure is practically the same, of course.

Such an example can be extended to other occupations. If all parties were equal to the challenge, we could use the reduction in working hours, the transfer of bonus payments from money to time off and the creation of conditions suitable for 'individual working hours' to stem the tide of unemployment.

It will not be easy. We cannot ignore the fact that today's consumer society encourages greed and the ability to succeed even at the expense of others. The concepts of turning away from a wrong direction and of sharing what is available lie at the heart of the Christian tradition. But it is much easier to make a scapegoat of the state, the employers, the employees or some other combination, than to commit ourselves individually and collectively to helping solve the problem. This means making sacrifices and abandoning our rights. Erich Fromm has written that for the first time in history the existence of man depends on a radical change of heart. We will not solve our problem at a cheaper price.

This article is extracted from the French monthly *Changer* and appeared in *New World News* 30 April 1983

The *Lebenshaus* in Trossingen

Lebenshaus Ökumenische Gemeinschaft Für Soziale Integration [The House of Life Ecumenical Community for Social Integration]

The beginnings

At the beginning of the nineteen eighties, the Christian peace movement had fallen into a crisis of meaning when it became apparent that even the public outcry and all their activities against so-called rearmament would not lead to the desired goal, and that the then approved deployment of medium-range missiles in the Federal Republic was to be carried out after all — in spite of everything.

The Peace group, which eventually became the Lebenshaus in Trossingen, was in a somewhat better position than most at the time. Since it was located in a rural area (at the eastern edge of the Black Forest, the Baar and the western edge of the Swabian Alb), it had long before the big crisis agreed to meet at least once a month rotating on a Sunday in a private apartment and to address together topics that went beyond the non-violent resistance to the planned missile installation. By the way, this monthly meeting still takes place today, mainly due to the perseverance of Ullrich Hahn.

Thus, the people in this group were not just opposing a particular cause. It quickly became clear to most of them that it was also of great importance to actually be for something and to make it their task to overcome social grievances. Thus began the search for such a task, which should be appropriate to the resources available and at the same time community-building in the sense of promoting the emergence of a community of solidarity. This search took some time, and after initial discussions about the creation of an inpatient hospice, the group finally agreed not to specialize and create a "house of death" but rather a "house of life" that would be open to people of both sexes and all ages in need of help, people who could not or did not want to live alone. The only criteria for admission should be that there should be hope that a stay in the Lebenshaus would be helpful for the person in question on his or her path through life (the so-called "perspective") and that the admission of these persons should appear reasonable to the people already living in the house. People who need inpatient therapy were to be excluded (there was no thought of a therapeutic residential community), as were addicted people, including those who had undergone withdrawal in hospital. This was not and is not about discriminating against such people. Rather, it was clear that the people living in the house would not be able to provide the necessary professional help. In the same way, children and adolescents were to be excluded because they cannot determine their own lives and at the same time we did not want to have anything to do with the relevant state authorities. Incidentally, this has changed in the meantime: After persistent urging by the district youth welfare office in Tuttlingen, we finally agreed to provide a room for a maximum stay of three months at a time, in a sense for emergency admissions of young people until a permanent stay elsewhere is organized by the district youth welfare office.

In the preparatory phase, the group of friends visited and inspected various institutions and spoke with several experts to finally arrive at a concept for a project that would close a gap in the public social care system and have a prospect of permanence. One statement remained in the memory and shaped all future activities: Relationships between people today only have a chance of lasting longer if both sides make an effort to offer the respective partner both freedom and security.

These two concepts became a guideline not only for the internal structure of the planned house, but also for the organizational structure of the sponsoring group, as will be explained later.

Dr. Harald and Elvira König, who had been in overseas development service in Africa for many years and at that time had recently been living in Trossingen (he as a doctor in the Bethel rehabilitation clinic in Trossingen) agreed right at the beginning to move into the planned Lebenshaus together with their children (they have three sons). However, for the sake of the desired freedom, it seemed necessary to distribute the responsibility for the house and people living in it on more shoulders, the so-called core group, i.e. to have more than two adults as bearers of this responsibility. From the circle of friends at that time, no one else was willing and able to take on this co-responsibility on site, that is, in the house itself. Fortunately, two other physicians, Dr. Wolfgang and Dr. Ursula Steuer, joined the group of friends at a very early stage. They had also been in overseas development service in Africa for many years and now declared themselves willing to move in together with their children (at first two, later three), if it would be possible to find gainful employment for them at a reasonable distance from the house. The house was to be run and administered on a voluntary basis. By the way, this is still the case today. In the meantime, however, Dr. Steuer has moved out with his family.

A position fortunately became available at the rehabilitation clinic in Trossingen, where Harald König was employed. Dr. Wolfgang Steuer thus found his workplace, where he is still employed to this day.

Dr. Angelika Braselmann, a single young doctor, joined them later, so that during the best times the so-called core group consisted of five adults. Nowadays there are the König couple and Mrs. Braselmann, so there are three.

Angelika Braselmann was in the meantime in overseas development service in Peru and now works in the Nudelhaus.

Whereas the people of the so-called core group live in the Lebenshaus for as long as possible—usually for many years—the duration of stay for the other house residents is limited. Originally, an upper limit of one year was considered, but it became apparent quite soon that in many cases this was too short, e.g. if a person lives in the house and wants/is supposed to undergo training (apprenticeship) that lasts three to four years, In such cases, the stay is assured for its duration. On the other hand, the stay can be very short; I remember a young woman who spent only one night in the house. Apparently, that was enough for her to learn all that she should and wanted to learn.

Six to eight rooms are available for the other residents, depending on the composition of the core group. These are all single rooms, in order to ensure that people can retreat into their own private space. The only exception is the admission of single parents, who usually have their small children with them in their own room.

After it was clear that the König couple would take over the main responsibility in the house and were willing to live there, the search for a suitable building was focused on

Trossingen. Finally, we found a former office and factory building that belonged to the town, which sold it to us. A supporting association was founded for this purpose, which has been the owner of the house ever since. All residents of the house, including the core group, pay rent and proportional living expenses.

The association has a board of directors, which is elected every two years at the annual general meeting. The board consists of the first and the deputy chairman, the treasurer, the secretary and the assessors. Board meetings are held once a month and are open to members.

Although members of the core group do not have the right to stand for election, i.e. cannot be members of the Board of Management, they regularly attend the Board of Management meetings and participate in the decision-making process.

In addition to the Board of Directors, there are the following committees within the association:

Supervision group consisting of the board and particularly committed members of the association under the leadership of an experienced theologian and psychotherapist who has been doing this work in the Lebenshaus in Trossingen for more than fifteen years. Here, above all, problems with the house residents and among the house residents are discussed.

Admission committee with an ideal composition of half the members of the core group and half of the external group of friends, whereby the core group naturally has a right of veto. This is where the preliminary decision is made as to which applicants will be admitted. The final decision is formally made by the board of directors; however, as a rule, the course has already been set in the supervision circle.

After originally holding a Bible study every Friday evening and an open evening every last Saturday of the month, interest and participation in them have diminished over the years. As a consequence, both events have been merged in the meantime and held on the last Friday of each month. Of course, there is still time and possibility for any other events at other times.

Once a year, the board of directors, together with particularly committed members of the association, goes on a weekend retreat to discuss fundamental issues.

By 1987, the remodeling of the building had been essentially completed, and the Lebenshaus in Trossingen was able to begin its work. It had already become clear after a few years that one of the main difficulties for those admitted was to find and hold down a job for gainful employment so that they could essentially earn their own living expenses. The efforts of the members of the association to find such jobs were not successful to a sufficient extent, which is why the so-called Nudelhaus was finally set up in another building acquired by the association, mainly through the work of Elvira König.

The Nudelhaus, after more than ten years of successful operation, now employs around fifteen people on a full- and part-time basis and covers its own costs, including appropriate wages and salaries. On the upper two floors there are rooms and apartments which are rented out at a reasonable price and for some people provide a step towards greater independence.

The purchase, conversion and furnishing of both houses cost around two million marks.

These funds were raised mainly through donations, especially from the state and "Aktion Sorgenkind" (now called "Aktion Mensch") and through private interest-free loans from association members and friends. Fortunately, we did not need bank loans from the house bank in Trossingen in the beginning, only the GLS (an anthroposophical bank) helped us with low-interest loans.

The emergence of a community of solidarity bore fruit, especially in the first few years. Many of the group of friends have taken out a so-called "loss of earnings insurance policy", i.e. they are prepared to support others financially in the event of loss of earnings. I myself was a beneficiary of this solidarity for many years.

For several years after I left industry, I received between one thousand and fifteen hundred marks a month from a solidarity fund set up and continually replenished by this group.

If it is a question of classifying the community that has been created and is emerging, it would probably be described as a kind of "surplus community", in which personal income and its use is a matter for the individual(s) and not for the group. Common projects are approached and financed according to the possibilities and the decision of these people. The same applies to the assets of the individual(s). The right to individual free disposal, not just once but again and again, is valued and respected very highly.

The Pioneer Society

On the occasion of the 10th anniversary of Lebenshaus Schwäbische Alb e.V. in 2004

It is my conviction that the biblical tradition of God's people is today (mostly unconsciously) carried on and supported by an "insightful minority", whereby it is irrelevant whether this has religious roots or not (I personally would regret it if it has none, because then everything certainly becomes incomparably more difficult). In this tradition, which was obviously also decisive for Jesus, the majority thinking, which is usual in the occidental tradition for political effectiveness, is turned upside down. With images like light, salt, leaven, city on the hill, as with the idea of God's people, according to this tradition, there is talk of tiny minorities that ultimately change the world. This minority becomes the vehicle on which—now again expressed in religious terms—God introduces his ideas into the world and these ultimately become a reality—above all, actually, through imitation. This is not, therefore, what we expect from the great political majorities.

For this "discerning minority", the task today is to show the limits of individualism and to develop communities of solidarity in which contemporary man can experience freedom and security, two of his basic needs. This is what is attempted with the *Lebenshäuser*. Of course, these are not the only valid attempts. There may well be many ways to do this, but they certainly represent a valid attempt.

And Gammertingen is without a doubt one of them.

It is extraordinarily gratifying that the various *Lebenshäuser* and similar communities that have formed in recent years have very different emphases. For example, Gammertingen, characterized above all by Michael Schmid and Katrin Warnatzsch, has focused more strongly than the other institutions of this kind, on the one hand, on the question of violence and the associated armament madness and, on the other hand, on the integration of refugees coming to Germany from all over the world, that is, of solidarity with foreigners. "Let many flowers bloom." This sentence is attributed to Mao Tse Tung. For Gammertingen, this means — correctly — peace work and refugee work.

It goes without saying that this also raises the question of justice — especially justice in the global economy — and the question of money and its multiplication through interest and compound interest, as well as the question of property.

A Last Thought

This short essay was written in May 2004 just prior to his death three months later.

The question of God's gracious goodness has been raised in the most diverse forms since its very beginnings. That in spite of all transgressions, a merciful God also accepts a lost soul after death.

The influence of Judaism initially played a formative role. This involved the question of a merciful God, whose conception is rooted in Judaism. Indeed, the question arises whether a warm-hearted relationship with God is possible without the sacrificial death of Jesus on Golgotha.

In Judaism, the idea of an unconditionally gracious God reaches its climax in the Kabala, where with the Shechina an image is disseminated that is already significant in the oral tradition of Judaism and without which a sacrificial theology in Christianity is, despite everything, an impossibility. But a gracious God is conceivable without the image of the sacrificial death of Jesus on the cross, that indeed the death on the cross is superfluous for a gracious God. The fact that the altar plays a major role in Christian dogma does not change this. It is still a sacrificial table and serves to appease the deity.

The whole question of hell and purgatory emerges and requires an answer in order to arrive at a conclusion on the question of sacrificial theology. Ultimately, the issue is whether God is a punishing God and whether the actions of man are ultimately sacrifices to appease God in the face of human transgressions against God's "laws".

More Books in English by Wilhelm Haller

Neither Sword nor Scepter

In his revolutionary book, Neither Sword nor Scepter, Wilhelm Haller (1935-2004) discusses justice in our economic system and in our society. In doing so, he brings into play quite original approaches to solutions based on an almost completely forgotten idea.

Known as the inventor of flexitime and as the author of several books and numerous articles on management, economics and theological topics, he saw himself as a student of Martin Buber and Hugh J. Schonfield.

But he also speaks from a rich life experience as entrepreneur and founder of several social projects.

This book has hitherto only been published in German. This English interpretation now makes it available to a wider range of readers. Although written in the 1990s, its message is just as relevant and pertinent today. It is of interest not only to the manager and business leader but also to politicians and all those who have an interest in the why's and wherefore's of our society.

The Dark Fire — God's Destructive and Loving Power in Man

God's Destructive and Loving Power in Man

The incarnation of God does not only refer to his Light Side, which for us Christians is represented in Jesus. Also, the dark side of God, for many manifested in the devil, chooses man as his home, and it is crucially important for man to become aware of this fact. Here lies a great mystery, which probably cannot be fully fathomed in one human life. And yet, in view of the massive threat to man and nature in our time, we must face up to this question ... Man is an autonomous, self-sufficient, independent being, whose task it is to go his own way, alone and with the help of his fellow men, in good and evil. He acts on his own responsibility. God gives him the strength to do so. He fulfils his own.

Available in Texianer Verlag, Tuningen
www.texianer.com